So Long, Snowman

Tana Reiff

GLOBE PEARSON

Pearson Learning Group

LifeTimes™ Titles

So Long, Snowman
The Family from Vietnam
A Time to Choose
Mollie's Year
Juan and Lucy
A Place for Everyone
The Shoplifting Game

Editorial Director: Robert G. Bander
Managing Designer: Kauthar Hawkins
Cover, text design, and illustrations: Wayne Snyder and
    Teresa Snyder

ISBN 0-8224-4321-X

Printed in the United Stated of America
7 8 9 10 11   05 04 03 02

Globe
Fearon

Pearson Learning Group

1-800-321-3106
www.pearsonlearning.com

Contents

CHAPTER 1

I have
a lot of time
to think now.
I just sit around
and think.
All day,
every day.
I think most
about the past.
I think and think,
and then I write.
By the way,
my name is Billy.

My troubles started
in high school.
Well, maybe they started
long before then.
You see,
when I was a kid,
I was bad.

I always
got into trouble
over little things.
But then
I got to high school.
And my troubles
got real big.
They've stayed big
ever since.
I guess
I just have a way
of walking
into trouble.

I grew up
on the South Side.
When I was a kid,
I didn't know anything
but that place.
It's pretty bad there.
But I didn't know
how bad it was.
It was home to me.

My mom
tried to make me right.

She really did.
I guess
it was hard for her.
I didn't have a dad.
Most kids I knew
didn't have a dad.
I never was around
a real man.
Oh, I saw
some good men.
But not in my house.
So how could I learn
to be one?

Now I'm a man.
Or so the law says.
And now I must learn
how to be good at it.
So far
I'm not doing very well.

Thinking It Over

1. From where do you think Billy is writing this?

2. Do you think someone can just "walk into trouble"? Why or why not?

3. What do you think of what Billy said about men?

CHAPTER 2

I will never forget
my last day
of high school.

I hated school.
I hated the principal.
I hated all the teachers.
They all hated me, too.

I hated the work
they made us do.
I didn't care
one little bit
about history
and George Washington
and Egypt.
But that's all
they gave us.
They never let us
do what we wanted to do.
They never told us

how to be
good card players.
They never told us
how to pick up girls.
They never told us
how to drink all night.
They never told us
where to find good pot.
And that's all
I wanted to know
back then.

So all us brothers
hung around together.
We gave everyone trouble.
Nothing but trouble.
I got kicked out of school
10 times.
First I got kicked out
for giving lip
to a teacher.
Then I got kicked out
for lighting a fire
in a wastebasket.
Then I got kicked out
for fighting.

You name it—
I got kicked out for it.

But the last time
was heavy.
Things at school
were just starting
to get better.
That was because
a music teacher
was teaching me
to play the horn.

Then one day someone stole
another teacher's coat.
It was not me.
But the other teacher *knew*
it was me.
She tried
to talk to me
real nice.

"I know you did it, Billy,"
said the teacher.
"Maybe we can
work this out."

"No way,"
I said.
"Because, Miss Teacher,
I did not do it!"

She kept saying
I took her coat.
I kept saying
I did not
take her coat.

Then I hit her
across the side
of her face.
She was a little thing.
She fell down
and hit her nose
on the desk.
Her glasses flew off
and broke.
There was blood
all over the place.

Just then
the principal came in.
I knew

for sure that
my school days
were over.

Thinking It Over

1. How did (do) you feel
    about school?
    Why?

2. What would you do
    if someone said
    you did something
    that you didn't do?

CHAPTER 3

I was only 15
when I got kicked out of school
for the last time.
They put me out
on the street
at 15.
I might have learned *something*
if I had stayed.
I might have
learned to really
play the horn.
Well, maybe they had to
kick me out.
I was bad news.

So there I was.
No school,
no job,
and my mom on welfare.
My mom
was real mad at me.

She said,
"You get out
and get a job!"
She must have said that
100 times a day.

And I always said,
"Sure, where am I
going to find a job?
There aren't any jobs!"

I did try
to find a job.
But no one wanted me.
Who would want a kid
who got kicked out of school
for hurting a teacher?

So I watched
a lot of TV.
I drank beer.
I smoked pot.
I hung out
on the street.
I just didn't have
anything better to do.

Thinking It Over

1. Do you think kids
   like Billy
   should get kicked out
   of school?
   Why or why not?

2. Is it hard
   to find a job?
   Why? Why not?

3. What would you do
   with your time
   if you couldn't find a job?

CHAPTER 4

There was
always something happening
on the street.
Even nothing
was something
on the street.

There was an old bar
called the North Pole.
It had boards
over the windows.
It looked
like it was closed down.
But it wasn't.
My friends and I
used to wait outside
for men to get us beer.
We were not old enough
to go in
and buy it ourselves.
We stood there

drinking beer
and shooting craps
and batting the bull
all day.
I guess we thought
it was fun.
It was better
than going to school
all day.

My friends and I
met in front of the North Pole
to make plans, too.
We started to rob
houses and stores uptown
at night.
Then some men in a truck
would meet us.
They took everything
we had:
TV's, CB's,
you name it.
They gave us money
for the stuff.
And then we bought
beer and pot.

And I bought a horn.
Hear me right!
I didn't steal it.
I bought
the best horn around.
Oh, how I loved
to play that horn!

We took
a lot of stuff.
But not many of us
got caught.
Some did.
But not me.
Not Billy.
No, I would never
get my tail caught.
I was too smart.

Thinking It Over

1.   What do you know
      about street life?

2.   Is there a way
      to keep out of trouble
      on the street?
      If so, how?
      If not, why not?

3.   What is the best thing
      you ever bought
      for yourself?

CHAPTER 5

It's real easy
to break into a house.
Take it from Billy—
if you have anything
worth money,
watch it.
It's really not that hard
to steal.
You just need to be cool.

We went out
to hit a house
on the West Side.
Nice houses—
and no one home.
And no dog.
The dog was
with the people.

When you break
into a house,

you've got to be careful.
If you hear
a bell ringing,
you better
get out of there fast.
The bell means
the cops are coming.

We broke a window
on the first floor.
No bell.
So two of us
went inside.
We looked around.
Everything was cool.
The other two boys
waited outside.
They came around
to the back door.
We handed them the TV.
They put it in the car.
We handed them the radio
and the record player.
They put those in the car.
That's all we wanted.
We knew we could get

quick money
for stuff like that.

We couldn't believe it!
It had been too easy—
no bell!
We got in the car.
We started down the driveway.
It was real dark.
We kept the car lights off
so no one
would see us.

We got to the end
of the driveway.
A car was
right there at the end.
It was parked sideways.
The car's lights went on.

It was a cop.

Thinking It Over

1. What can you do
    to keep from having
    your house robbed?

2. How do you feel
    the police can help
    if you have been robbed?

3. How can you help
    the police?

CHAPTER 6

This house
had a new way
to catch robbers.
As soon as
we broke the window,
a bell went off
for the cops.
It rang at the station.
We didn't hear it.

We were just having fun.
We didn't want to
hurt people.
We didn't even have guns.

Since I was only 16,
they didn't
put me in jail.
They put me
in a home
for bad boys.

It was called Boys' Hall.
It was bad.
They wouldn't let us
go anywhere.

I looked at old magazines
and watched TV a lot.
I just sat around
all day long.
Some boys stayed in bed
all day and all night.
The food was bad—
lots of beans.

Sometimes people came
to visit.
They brought cookies.
Cookies!
But no one ever came
to visit me.
Only the probation officer.

But I got to know
a lot of the people there.
I even knew
some of them before.

We talked about
why we were in Boys' Hall.
We talked about
what we were going to do
when we got out.
We got to be
good friends.

Thinking It Over

1. What should be done
   for young people
   who break the law?

2. Why do some people think
   that stealing is fun?

CHAPTER 7

A lot of the boys
in Boys' Hall
were on real bad trips.
Even worse than mine.
But one boy was cool.
His name was Willard.
His thing had been
stealing cars.
But he said it was
a dead end.
He had been caught
eight times.
Now he was finished.

"No more nights
in this hotel," he said.
He seemed
to mean it.

Willard asked me
about myself.

First I told him
about my horn.
Then I talked about
stealing and pot.

"Man," he said.
"You've really got something
going for you.
But you don't even know it."

I asked him,
"What do you mean?"

"The problem is money—right?
Well, that horn of yours is
a ticket
to big money.
If you play it right,"
he said.

"I don't understand,"
I told him.

"Billy," said Willard.
"Where's the big money
when you play it clean?

At sports games
and in night clubs.
When you rip people off,
you make them feel bad.
They don't like that.
But when you play your horn
real sweet,
you make people feel good.
And lots of people
pay big money
just to feel good."

   "But I just fool around,"
I said.
"I never had real lessons.
I just play."

   "You don't know
what you can do
until you do it.
Do you think that
Chuck Mangione
was born with a horn
in his mouth?
He *learned* to play it.
You can, too."

Willard gave me
a lot to think about.
I wanted to get
my hands on my horn
so bad I could taste it.

Thinking It Over

1. What is the difference
    between *learning*
    and *playing around?*

2. What can make people
    really change their ways,
    not just talk about doing it?

CHAPTER 8

When the other boys and I
got out of Boys' Hall,
we were good friends.
We went to see each other
all the time.
All but Willard.
He moved away.
I still thought about him
once in a while.
At first I remembered
what he had told me.
But after a while
I forgot it.
I never saw Willard again.

Some of the boys
from the Hall
got into hard drugs.
One called Snowman
saw me on the street
one day.

"Say, Billy!
Come on up
to my place
and get a rush,"
the Snowman said.

"What kind of rush
are you talking about?"

"Junk, man,"
he said.
"Heroin. Smack.
Costs less than snow.
What else would I mean?"

I had been heading home
to play my horn.
But I said,
"OK, Snowman.
Where do you live?"

We walked up
to his place
on the third floor.
No one was home.
His mom was at work.

He showed me his works.
I had seen works before,
and these were not very cool.
But I took off my shirt.
And I got turned on to junk
for the first time.
I got real high.
I dug it.
Snowman and I
just sat back
and listened to music
all day.

And that was
just the first day
like that.

Thinking It Over

1. What do you do
    to have a good time?

2. Can good times
    sometimes go bad?
    Why?

3. Why can some people
    learn to say no
    when others can't?

CHAPTER 9

I knew
you could get junk
anywhere.
You just had to have
some money.
I wanted to turn on again.
But I didn't
have any money.
I wasn't
good enough
to play my horn
for people yet.

So I had
only one way
to get money.
That way was stealing—
the way
I got caught
the last time.
You couldn't make real money

on a job—
even if you had one.

So my friends and I
played Spot and Steal.
We'd drive around
all day and spot.
At night
we'd go out and steal.
We sold more stuff
to the men
who came around for it.
Some stuff
we sold ourselves.
We made more money
by selling it ourselves.

I used to spend my money
on beer and pot
and cool clothes.
That was before I went
to Boys' Hall.
Now I spent my money
on drugs only.
Getting drugs
was my only thing.

It took all the money
I could get.
I needed it
more and more.
I could just about
get it together
to steal enough
to keep up.

We started
to rob stores.
We had to be real careful
about stores—
they all had bells.
I sure didn't want
to get caught again.

But I did get caught.

It was
back to Boys' Hall
for me.
And they don't
give you drugs
at Boys' Hall.

Thinking It Over

1. What do *you* think
   is a good way
   to get money?

2. Why might a person
   make the same mistake
   two times?

3. Why do drugs and stealing
   sometimes go together?

CHAPTER 10

I didn't
have to tell
the people at Boys' Hall
I was on drugs.
They could tell
right away.

They wanted
to get me off drugs
real fast.
I wanted that too.
Really, I did.
So they sent me
to the hospital.
It was a real bad time
for a while.
I got real sick.
I was in bad shape.
I didn't know
what was going on
or what was happening to me.

I thought
I was going to die.

Everyone was trying
to help me.
The thing was,
I didn't want their help.
I was feeling real mean.

My mom was mad
at the whole thing.
She kicked me
out of the house.
She said,
"Take all your things
and get out.
I don't want
to see you."

So when I got out
of Boys' Hall,
I moved in
with this girl
named Sandy.
She was 19.
I was 17.

Sandy had a job.
She also had a baby.
Sandy was real nice to me.
So when she went to work,
I took care of the baby,
even though it wasn't mine.
And I played my horn
as much as I could.
Sandy sure did like
the way I played it.
I got better at it, too.

But I still
got into trouble.
Snowman and the boys
came over
when Sandy was at work.
They got me high.
I tried
to stay off drugs.
But it's real hard
to stay clean
on South Side.

Willard had made it
sound so simple.

Well, it wasn't simple.
But one thing I knew
for sure.
If Willard was still around,
it would be easy
to break with Snowman.

Thinking It Over

1. Have you ever known
   anyone who was trying
   to get off drugs?

2. Why do you think
   it's so hard
   for Billy
   to stay off drugs?

3. What would you do
   if you were Billy's mom?

CHAPTER 11

Sandy didn't know
about the drugs
at first.
Then she started
to see the marks
on my arms and legs.

She was mad about it.
But she didn't
kick me out.
See, Sandy was going to have
another baby.
And this time
it *was* my baby.

"Billy,
you better get clean,"
said Sandy.
"Soon I'll have to
stop working.
You're going to have to

get a job
and earn some money.
We will need it.
I can't work
much longer."

   "Oh, sure,"
I said.
"I couldn't get a job
two years ago.
I got kicked out of school.
I have a police record.
I'm on drugs.
Who would take me now?"

   Well, Sandy worked
at a restaurant.
She told them
a little bit
about our problems.
She asked them
to give me a job.

   They were
pretty cool about it.
They didn't ask

a lot of questions
about my past.
They just told me
I had to work hard.
So they gave me a job
washing dishes.
It wasn't much,
but it was something.
It was the first job
I had ever had.
The first real job,
that is.

The baby came
in December.
It was a boy.
He was beautiful.
My own little baby boy.
We named him James.

I just had to show James
to my mom.
I took him over
to her place.
She cried.
She laughed.

She took James
in her arms
and held him.

I asked her,
"How do you like him?"

"He's beautiful, Billy,"
said my mom.
"He's as beautiful a baby
as you were."

I looked
at little James.
I hope
you do better in life
than your old man,
I thought.

Thinking It Over

1. If you had a restaurant,
   would you give Billy a job?
   Why or why not?

2. Why did Billy
   take a job now,
   when he wouldn't before?

3. Think of a child
   you have hopes for.
   What things must happen
   for hopes to become real?

CHAPTER 12

My mom
really dug James.
She said
she would take care of him
and Sandy's other kid
if Sandy wanted
to go back to work.
Mom even told me
she missed me
and my old horn.
She didn't know that
I didn't have much time
for the horn
these days.

The restaurant
was nice enough
to take Sandy back.
So she worked.
And I worked.
And my mom

took care of the kids
during the day.

Things were
going along pretty good.
I still saw Snowman
from time to time.
I still got high,
but I don't think
I was hooked.
I kept my works
where Sandy would
never find them.

One night
I was at work.
Sandy got it
in her head
to check up on me.
She started to look
through my things.
She found the works.

After work
I went out
for a drink.

I had more than one.
By the time
I got home
I was pretty drunk.
Not mean.
Just drunk.

It was real late.
I saw that
the lights were on.
That's funny,
I thought.
Sandy's not in bed yet.
I thought maybe
something was wrong
with James.

When I got
to the door,
Sandy opened it.
She was real mad.
She was holding the works
in her hand.

She asked,
"What is this?"

I knew
I was in for trouble.
But I didn't know
how much.

Thinking It Over

1. Why is good child care
   important for busy parents?

2. Do you think
   there's ever a good reason
   to look through
   someone else's things?
   Why or why not?

3. If you feel trouble coming,
   what do you do?

CHAPTER 13

Sandy asked again,
"What is this?"

I said,
"What does it look like?"

"Have you
been doing junk?"
Sandy looked at me.

"No," I lied.
I just didn't want her
to know about it.
I looked down.
She knew I had lied.

She threw the works
in my face.

"Hold it, Sandy.
Stay cool.

Stay cool."
I knew
she was very, very mad
about finding the works.

"I should have known,"
she said.
"I've been wondering
why there isn't any money
when we're both working.
You've been buying drugs.
That's why."

Then I got really mad.
At least
I wasn't selling drugs.
Why didn't she see that?
I grabbed her arm.

Sandy shouted,
"Get your hands off me!"

I grabbed her other arm.
I pulled both arms
behind her back.
Then I kicked her.

She fell down
on the floor.
She cried.

I heard James crying
in the other room.

Sandy got up.
She wanted to run out.
I grabbed her again.
I'm a lot stronger
than she is.
A lot stronger.

Then we were out
in the hall.
People opened their doors
to see what was going on.

Sandy started
for the steps.
But I still
held on to her.
I hit her
across the face.
She hit me back.

I hit her again.
She fell.
And she couldn't catch hold
of anything.
I saw her fall
down the steps.
I saw her go down
one step at a time.
It happened very fast.

I looked down.
She was at
the bottom
of the steps.
But didn't move.
I felt sick.
I hadn't wanted to hurt her.
I loved her.
Why had I done that?

I heard police cars
coming up the street.

Thinking It Over

1. Do you think a person
    should ever lie
    to keep from hurting
    someone?
    Why or why not?

2. Have you ever been
    really angry?
    What did you do?

3. What would you do
    if you saw a bad fight
    going on?

CHAPTER 14

Sandy will be OK.
Thank God.
They put her
in the hospital.
She was hurt pretty bad.
But she will be OK.

I told the cops
to take the kids
to my mother.
She knows how
to take care of them.

And me?
Guess where I am.
I'm in jail.
Yes, a real live jail.
With bars and police
all over the place.
I turned 18
two weeks ago.

No more Boys' Hall
for me.
I'm a man of 18 now.

They gave me
a lawyer.
We go to court soon.
I don't know
what will happen
to me now.

So I sit
here in jail
and think.
I don't really think
I'm a bad person.
Deep down,
I know I'm OK.
I just have to learn
to stay clean—somehow.

What is it?
Is it my home life?
Is it the South Side?
Is it boys like Snowman?
Is it me?

Is it everything?
What made me
do what I did?
Why am I
so bad?

   I've been
in a lot of trouble
for only being 18.
I hope
it doesn't get worse.
I hope
they go light on me.
I hope they
give me a break.

   And I hope
Sandy will
take me back.
Let me be her man.
I hope James will
let me be his dad.
I'll show them
I can say
so long to Snowman.
And Willard—

I read you loud and clear.
I'll play
my horn again.
I'll get real good at it.
You and everyone else
will want to hear me play.

   So that's my story
up to now.
It's not
a very good story.
Some day
I'll have better things
to write about.
Until then,
I have
a lot of work to do.
But just you wait.
I'll do it.

Thinking It Over

1. What control did Snowman
    have over Billy?
    Why?

2. What control did Willard
    have over Billy?
    Why?

3. How can Sandy and Billy
    get their lives back together?

4. Would you blame
    a person like Billy
    for all the things
    he has done?
    Some?
    Why?